A CHRISTIAN GUIDE
to the
BIBLICAL
FEASTS

DAVID WILBER

Freedom Hill Community
PO Box 1865, Saint Charles, MO 63302-1865 USA
www.freedomhillcommuntiy.com

Comments and questions: www.freedomhillcommunity.com

A CHRISTIAN GUIDE
to the
BIBLICAL FEASTS

DAVID WILBER

CONTENTS

INTRODUCTION
RETURNING TO GOD'S FEASTS

Let us therefore celebrate the festival.
— Paul, 1 Corinthians 5:8

The Bible records for us that all Scripture is breathed out by God and profitable for teaching, reproof, correction, and training in righteousness (2 Timothy 3:16). But many Christians today have forgotten some very important parts of Scripture—namely, the Sabbath and feasts of the Lord. While much of modern Christianity doesn't regard these commandments in the Torah (Law) as particularly relevant to our lives today, an awakening is taking place. Christians around the world are beginning to see the value in these ancient instructions and seeking to apply them to their lives.

Some might say, "But those parts of God's Law are done away with and no longer binding on Christians!" That is the common assertion made by Christians who object to the idea of returning to God's Sabbath and feasts. However, the arguments in support of this assertion are greatly lacking. The New Testament doesn't teach that God's Sabbath and feasts are irrelevant to Christians. Indeed, it teaches just the opposite!

The word *Christian* literally means "follower of Christ." As Christians, we are to walk as Christ walked (1 John 2:6). How did He walk? Well, many Christians might be surprised to discover that Yeshua (Jesus) lived His life as a Torah-observant Jewish believer. His followers called Him Rabbi, He rested on the Sabbath every seventh day, and He kept the biblical feast days. In his book, *Meet the Rabbis*, Professor of Biblical Literature, Dr. Brad Young, Ph.D., puts it this way:

> We too often view Jesus in a historical vacuum with the result that we transpose our twenty-first century Western values and concerns onto him. We tend to make him into a good Methodist, Catholic, Baptist, Anglican, Pentecostal, or whatever denominational orientation we may be. The historical Jesus remains a Jew. His faith and obedience to his Father in heaven had at its center the precious gift given at Mount Sinai: Torah.[1]

During His famous sermon on the mount, Yeshua (Jesus) made it very clear to His audience what He was doing with regard to the Torah and Prophets:

> Do not think that I have come to abolish the Law or the Prophets; I have not come to abolish them but to fulfill them. (Matthew 5:17)

Yeshua said, "Do not think." In other words, He didn't want there to be the slightest misunderstanding about His mission as it concerns

---

1   Dr. Brad Young, *Meet the Rabbis: Rabbinic Thought and the Teachings of Jesus* (Grand Rapids, MI: Baker Academic, 2010), p. 46.

the Torah. Indeed, He didn't want His audience to even consider the thought that He came to abolish it.

What does it mean to abolish the Torah?

In Greek, the word for "abolish" is kataluo, which means to "abrogate, destroy, nullify." It is often used to describe tearing down or smashing physical objects. Yeshua used this word when He prophesied the destruction of the Temple (Matthew 24:2). The word is also used in a figurative way to mean "render useless" (Acts 5:38). So we are not to think that Yeshua came to destroy the Torah—that is, nullify it or make it void.

What does it mean to fulfill the Torah?

First, let's discuss what fulfilling the Torah doesn't mean. Obviously, it can't mean to "abrogate, destroy, nullify" because that's what abolish means. However, some understand this part of Yeshua's statement to mean that He "completed" the Torah and Prophets in such a way that parts of the Torah—like the Sabbath and feasts—no longer have a literal application in the lives of Christians, which we're told is somehow different from abolishing them. But this idea poses several problems.

First of all, Yeshua exhorts His followers to "do" and "teach" the commandments of the Torah (Matthew 5:19). It wouldn't make sense for Yeshua to exhort Christians to do and teach the Commandments in the Torah in this passage if He voided parts of it by fulfilling it. Second, Yeshua's mission to fulfill refers to not only the Torah, but also the Prophets. So if we're going to say that the Torah no longer applies to our lives, we must say the same about the words of the Prophets—but obviously that would be absurd. And last, the very next verse says that not an iota or dot—that is, the smallest letter or stroke—will pass from the Torah until heaven and earth pass away and all is accomplished:

> For truly, I say to you, until heaven and earth pass away, not
> an iota, not a dot, will pass from the Law until all is accom-
> plished. (Matthew 5:18)

Yeshua appeals to the created universe as a standard for the ongoing validity of the Torah. The *Tanakh* (Old Testament) often uses the created universe in the same way to demonstrate the validity of God's Word and promises (Psalm 89:36-37; Jeremiah 31:35-36; 33:20-21). Thus, the created universe confirms the validity of even the smallest letter of the Torah. Yeshua makes a similar statement in the Gospel of Luke:

> It is easier for heaven and earth to pass away than for one dot
> of the Law to become void. (Luke 16:17)

Scholars have suggested that heaven and earth passing away refers to the close of our present age. In the Cornerstone Biblical Commentary on the Gospel of Matthew, Dr. David L. Turner puts it this way:

> The phrases "until heaven and earth disappear" and "until its
> purpose is achieved" [until all is accomplished, ESV] refer to
> the end of the present world and the beginning of the escha-
> ton. Until that time the law is valid. Matthew 5:19 goes on to
> infer from 5:18's statement of the perpetual authority of the
> law that it had better be obeyed and taught by disciples of the
> Kingdom. It would be hard to make a stronger statement of
> the ongoing authority of the Torah than is made in 5:18.[2]

---

2   Dr. David L. Turner, *Cornerstone Biblical Commentary: The Gospel of Matthew* (Carol
     Stream, IL: Tyndale House Publishers, Inc., 2005), p. 85.

Interestingly, Revelation 21-22 speaks of the day when heaven and earth will indeed pass away and all will be accomplished—that is, the close of our present age—and a new heaven and earth will be established. The passing of heaven and earth coincides with the end of crying, mourning, pain, and death (Revelation 21:4). Since crying, mourning, pain, and death still exist in our current age, it follows that nothing from the Torah has passed away.

So then what does Yeshua mean when He says He came to fulfill the Torah? In looking at the overall context, some commentators have suggested that "fulfill" in this passage means to establish or confirm. A plain reading of the text certainly favors this interpretation. Yeshua came to fulfill the Torah and Prophets (5:17); the Torah is valid and not a single part of it will pass away until the created universe passes away (5:18); Yeshua's followers will do and teach even the least of the commandments in the Torah (5:19); and members of the kingdom of heaven are identified by their righteousness, which is according to the Torah and Prophets (5:20). Thus, the concept of fulfilling the Torah and Prophets is unpacked in the following verses to include doing and teaching the commandments. Furthermore, the scribes and Pharisees are given as the standard of righteousness that disciples of Yeshua must surpass. Why? Because they are known for their observance of the least of the Torah commandments.

Thus, Yeshua did not come to render the Torah void, but to fully do and teach the Torah and establish it in the lives of His followers. In his commentary on this passage in Matthew, J.K. McKee puts it this way:

> When Yeshua came to "fulfill the Law," it was with the ex-
> pressed intention to demonstrate how valuable the Torah is
> for the instruction of the faithful, because His very sermon on
> the Mount is predicated upon the validity of Moses' Teaching

> [...] Yeshua the Messiah, as the Word of God made manifest
> in the flesh (John 1:1), came to fulfill the Torah for humanity
> by embodying it to its fullest extent in His teachings, actions,
> and deeds.[3]

Indeed, our Messiah's statement in Matthew 5:17-20 is clear. The text does not indicate anywhere that Yeshua intended to nullify any of the commands of Torah by fulfilling them. The implications of Yeshua's declarative statement, therefore, is that we as Christians ought to still be following the Torah—including the Sabbath and feasts!

That being the case, it shouldn't surprise us to see that the early Christians continued to follow the Torah even long after Yeshua's resurrection. Indeed, we have clear references in the Scriptures that the early Christians continued to keep and teach the Sabbath (Acts 13:14, 42, 44; 16:13; 17:1-2; 18:4), Passover (Acts 20:6; 1 Corinthians 5:6-8; 11:23-29), Shavuot/Pentecost (Acts 2:1; 20:16; 1 Corinthians 16:8), Yom Kippur/Day of Atonement (Acts 27:9), and Sukkot/Tabernacles (Acts 18:21). The apostles were merely following the instructions Yeshua gave them just prior to His ascension. He said to make disciples of all the nations and teach them all that He had commanded them (Matthew 28:19-20). *All* that He commanded them certainly included His teaching in Matthew 5:17-20, in which He affirmed the ongoing authority of the Sabbath and feasts as part of the Torah. It wasn't until after the first century that most Christians began to neglect these biblical practices.

---

3   J.K. McKee, *The New Testament Validates Torah: Does the New Testament Really Do Away With the Law?* (Richardson, TX: Messianic Apologetics, 2012), p. 91.

Were the Sabbath and feasts given only to the Jewish people?

Some have rejected the idea that we are to keep the Sabbath and feasts because they see them as laws given only to Israel in order to set them apart from other nations. It is argued that Christians are not part of the covenant that God made with Israel; therefore, we are not required to keep some of the commandments given in the Torah.

Was God's intention really for only the Jewish people to keep the Sabbath and feasts? In his article, "Which day is the Sabbath?" Dr. Craig Keener, Ph.D., makes the following statement:

> As I tried to study the biblical text honestly, I could see that this was not just a matter of keeping laws designated for Israel; God actually modeled the Sabbath rest in creation (Gen 2:2-3). Whether we take that narrative literally or not, the principle of the Sabbath is there, and it apparently is an example for all people, not just those who are ethnically descended from Abraham.[4]

Interestingly, the fourth commandment passage itself mandates a Sabbath rest for not only Israel, but also "the sojourner" and even animals (Exodus 20:10). So even when the Sabbath is given within the context of God's covenant with Israel, the command to rest was not given to Israel exclusively. The sojourner was also instructed to rest on the Sabbath.

In addition, Isaiah 56:3-8 speaks of "the foreigner who has joined himself to the Lord." Scripture describes these foreigners as ones who keep the Sabbath and hold fast to the covenant. And because of that,

---

4   Dr. Craig Keener, *Bible Background: Research and Commentary by Dr. Craig Keener.* "Which day is the Sabbath?" www.craigkeener.com. Accessed 9/7/2016

God is pleased and they are promised an "everlasting name that shall not be cut off" (v. 5). This passage is a clear example of how God desires to be worshiped in His "house of prayer for *all* peoples" (v. 7, emphasis added).

As for the rest of the feast days, the sojourners, along with the native-born Israelites, were specifically commanded to keep Passover (Numbers 9:14), Unleavened Bread (Exodus 12:19), Yom Kippur (Leviticus 16:29), and Sukkot (Deuteronomy 16:14). So God expected not only native-born Israelites to keep His feasts, but everyone who worships the God of Israel to keep them.

It's clear that the Sabbath and feasts were not exclusive to native-born Israelites in the Old Testament. There's really no debate that everyone who called upon the name of the Lord was also to keep the Sabbath and feasts. But what about in the New Testament? Aside from where Paul instructs the church of Corinth, which would have included Gentiles, to keep the feast of Passover (1 Corinthians 5:7-8), Gentile believers are never explicitly commanded to keep the Sabbath or feasts in the New Testament. However, we cannot use that as our basis for saying that Gentile believers shouldn't keep them. The New Testament doesn't reiterate many commandments found in the Torah, such as "don't practice necromancy," yet Christians still believe we should keep them. Furthermore, Yeshua's instructions to His disciples were to make disciples of "all the nations" and teach them all that He had commanded them (Matthew 28:19-20), which would have included the Sabbath and feasts. Therefore, the Torah—including the Sabbath and feasts—is applicable doctrine for all who follow Yeshua, Jew and Gentile.

But didn't the apostles teach that it's okay to not keep the Sabbath and feasts?

Some have claimed that the Sabbath and feasts were fulfilled in Christ, which according to them means that we don't have to keep them anymore—at least not in the literal sense that the Bible describes. It is believed that Yeshua brought the Sabbath and feasts to a higher meaning in the New Covenant, which somehow annuls their practical application. Let's take a look at a few New Testament passages that are commonly used to support this theory.

> Matthew 12:1-2
> At that time Jesus went through the grainfields on the Sabbath. His disciples were hungry, and they began to pluck heads of grain and to eat. But when the Pharisees saw it, they said to him, "Look, your disciples are doing what is not lawful to do on the Sabbath."

Did Yeshua condone His disciples breaking the Sabbath in this passage? If so, wouldn't these verses demonstrate that the practical application of the Sabbath is fading away and it's not that important anymore in the New Testament?

First of all, as we've already seen, Yeshua completely affirms the validity of the Sabbath as part of the Torah in Matthew 5:17-20. Why would He condone His disciples breaking the Sabbath shortly after He affirmed it? Secondly, this dispute between Yeshua and the Pharisees was not about whether or not to keep the Sabbath; it was about *how* to keep the Sabbath. Yeshua's disciples were breaking the Sabbath only according to the Pharisees' *interpretation*. The Bible never prohibits plucking heads of grain on the Sabbath. Thus, Yeshua proclaimed his disciples "innocent" of wrongdoing (Matthew 12:7) and rebuked the Pharisees for missing the entire point of the Sabbath in their strict interpretations.

> Colossians 2:16-17
> Therefore let no one pass judgment on you in questions of food and drink, or with regard to a festival or a new moon or a Sabbath. These are a shadow of the things to come, but the substance belongs to Christ.

Is this passage saying that anyone who teaches obedience to the Sabbath and feasts is a judgmental legalist who emphasizes the "shadow" over the substance? Who are these judgmental people that Paul is warning against?

If we look earlier in the passage at Colossians 2:8, we see that Paul is warning the Colossian believers about those who are trying to lead them astray through deception and "human tradition." But the Sabbath and feasts are not human traditions. Moreover, these false teachings are said to be in opposition to the teachings of Messiah, but the Messiah affirms and teaches the Sabbath and feasts as part of the Torah. Indeed, Paul himself affirms the validity of the Sabbath and Feasts as part of "all Scripture" in 2 Timothy 3:16. As Tim Hegg explains in his book, *Why We Keep Torah: Ten Persistent Questions*, a more likely explanation is that these false teachers were judging the Colossian believers for *how* they kept the Sabbath and feasts:

> The point is that the false teachers are judging the Colossian believers in regard to their *halachah* in observing the Torah commandments relating to food, drink, festivals, new moons and the Sabbath. The false teachers are telling the Colossians that unless they observe the commandments in strict adher-

ence to their particular *halachah*, they are not actually keeping the commandments at all and will therefore fall under the judgment of God. It is the common Christian interpretation of these verses that Paul had taught the Colossian believers to disregard the Torah regulations of kosher foods and appointed times, and that the false teachers were trying to persuade them that these were necessary. But that interpretation neither fits the wider teaching of Paul nor the immediate context. The false teachers are suggesting that the Colossians are failing to observe the commandments as *they had determined they should be observe*d, not that the Colossians had entirely neglected the commandments.[5]

It's important to note what Paul does not say. He doesn't say that the Sabbath and feasts are now abolished or no longer literally applicable in the New Covenant. He was merely warning the Colossian believers against false teachers judging them with regard to how they observe certain commandments.

> Romans 14:5
> One man considers one day more sacred than another; another man considers every day alike. Each one should be fully convinced in his own mind.

Some Christians assume that Paul is referring to the Sabbath and feasts in this passage, but the Sabbath is never explicitly mentioned anywhere in the book of Romans. Since the text is unclear on the type of "day" being addressed in this passage, it is not necessary to conclude

---

5   Tim Hegg, *Why We Keep Torah: 10 Persistent Questions* (TorahResource, 2009), p. 64

that Paul must be referring to the Sabbath or feasts. Furthermore, the context of this verse is in regards to "opinions" or "disputable matters" (Romans 14:1). Surely in Scripture the Sabbath and feasts are never regarded as merely a matter of opinion.

So what exactly is Paul talking about when he says we must be fully convinced in our own mind when it comes to sacred days? In his commentary on this passage in Romans, J.K. McKee offers this explanation:

> Few consider the possibility that "eats" in 14:3 could be helping to introduce the sacred days specified in 14:5. When this is taken into consideration, we see that there were, in fact, various fixed days for fasting on the Jewish religious calendar, such as those remembering the fall of Jerusalem and destruction of the First Temple. I would submit that when "he who eats, does so for the Lord, for he gives thanks to God; and he who eats not, for the Lord he does not eat, and gives thanks to God" (14:6b, NASU), is discussing optional fast days, as opposed to eating meat—the second part of Paul's argument on disputable matters. Just as it would be inappropriate to judge fellow Believers who only eat vegetables, so would it also be inappropriate to judge fellow Believers who might observe special fast days for reasons that are very important to them.[6]

So the "opinions" over which days to hold sacred could have had to do with fast days, which would seem to fit better with the context. In either case, it's clear that this passage cannot be used to support the idea that the Sabbath and feasts are no longer important.

---

6   J.K. McKee, *Romans for the Practical Messianic* (Richardson, TX: Messianic Apologetics, 2014), p. 380

Galatians 4:10-11

Formerly, when you did not know God, you were enslaved to those that by nature are not gods. But now that you have come to know God, or rather to be known by God, how can you turn back again to the weak and worthless elementary principles of the world, whose slaves you want to be once more? You observe days and months and seasons and years! I am afraid I may have labored over you in vain.

For this passage, it's important to know some historical context. The Jewish people were not the only ones who observed "days and months and seasons." Paul is addressing former pagan idol worshipers who were coming out of these pagan cults that had their own times and seasons. In his commentary on Galatians, Tim Hegg gives the following insight:

> This interpretation, that Paul is referring to pagan days, months, seasons, and years fits best with the language he uses in which he speaks of the Gentiles as "turning back again" (*epistrefete*) to the weak and worthless elements. He has already identified their past as that of idolatry. To use the term "turn back again" for those whose former life was one of idolatry helps us identify that to which they were tempted to turn.[7]

Paul says that his audience was enslaved to these things "when they did not know God" (v. 8). Furthermore, Paul, an observant Jew, kept the Sabbath and feasts and certainly wouldn't consider them to be weak and worthless. Therefore, he couldn't possibly be referring to God's Sabbath and feasts in this passage.

---

7   Tim Hegg, *Paul's Epistle to the Galatians* (Tacoma, WA: TorahResource, 2010), p. 188

Wasn't the Sabbath changed to Sunday?

Around the second century, the practice of most Christian churches with regard to how and when to keep the Sabbath day had begun to change. It was taught that the Sabbath is no longer to be kept on the same day as in the Bible, but rather on Sunday. (It should be noted that not all Christians throughout history accepted this change. For instance, among other Christian groups, the Nazarenes continued to observe the Sabbath on the seventh day.) While it is true that Christian tradition since around the second century taught a Sunday Sabbath, our primary concern should be what the Bible teaches. As Tim Hegg says, "We cannot use history as the litmus test of truth, for God has not commanded us to conform to history, but to the unchanging standard of His word."[8] Is there any biblical basis for changing the Sabbath from the seventh day to Sunday? Only two verses in the New Testament are sometimes used to support this idea: Acts 20:7 and 1 Corinthians 16:2.

> Acts 20:7
>
> On the first day of the week, when we were gathered together to break bread, Paul talked with them, intending to depart on the next day, and he prolonged his speech until midnight.

Because this passage says that these early Christians gathered "on the first day of the week," some have argued that a shift from Sabbath observance to Sunday church occurred. But how exactly does that conclusion follow from a plain reading of the text? For all we know this could have just been a special one-time gathering put together because Paul was departing the next day. Why would we assume that

---

8   Tim Hegg, *TorahResource*. "It is Often Said: Two Thousand Years of Christianity Cannot be Wrong!" www.torahresource.com. Accessed 9/7/2016

this gathering took place every week? Moreover, why would we then make the leap in suggesting that this meeting implies a replacement of the Sabbath?

> 1 Corinthians 16:2
> On the first day of every week, each of you is to put something
> aside and store it up, as he may prosper, so that there will be
> no collecting when I come.

Again, why is it assumed that this is referring to the collection plate passed around at Sunday church services? The text doesn't suggest that this has anything to do with a meeting day. Paul is merely requesting that the Corinthian believers set aside savings as an offering to be sent to the saints in Jerusalem (v. 1). The instruction was for individual believers to put aside savings every week for this special offering so that when Paul arrived it would be available. The text doesn't indicate that these offerings were to be collected at a church service every week.

Conclusion

There appears to be no biblical basis for changing or ignoring the Sabbath or feast days. Nowhere in the Bible does God, Yeshua, or the apostles authorize their change or annulment. Rather, the disregard for the Sabbath and feasts in Christianity happened over time as Christians gradually drifted further and further away from the Jewish roots of their faith. Now that Christians around the world are returning to these ancient instructions, the most common question is, "How do I do this?" That's what the following chapters of this book will explore.

CHAPTER 1
THE SABBATH

Remember the Sabbath day, to keep it holy.
Exodus 20:8

When believers learn through the Scriptures that the Sabbath is still relevant for today, naturally what follows are many questions about what it means to follow this commandment. What does it mean to rest on the Sabbath and keep it holy? What should we do and not do on this day? The following is a list of ways that you and your family can incorporate the Sabbath into your lives.

Remember

We're told in Exodus 20:8 to *remember* the Sabbath day. That means don't forget about it! Thus, the first step in keeping this commandment is making the commitment to keep it. So throughout the other six days of the week, "remember" that on the seventh day you will be resting. When you make your plans, incorporate the Sabbath into your schedule. Don't make any plans on the seventh day that would take away from what you should be doing—that is, keeping the Sabbath. Just as the Lord has remembered His steadfast love and faithfulness to His people (Psalm 98:3), may we be faithful to Him and remember His Sabbath.

Rest/Don't Work

The Sabbath is to be kept every seventh day, which is from Friday sundown to Saturday sundown. (Biblical days begin in the evening.) On this day no work—that is, whatever you do for income and self-provision—is to be done (Exodus 20:10). This is because the Sabbath is ultimately a picture of our salvation in Messiah Yeshua, which is a gift from God and therefore cannot be "worked for." Just as the Sabbath is an opportunity for us to trust God for our physical provision, we must trust in Yeshua for our salvation. We cannot rely on our own efforts. God is the one who provides and we simply receive His blessings with grateful hearts.

In addition to not working ourselves, we are not to directly cause anyone else to work either. As the commandment says, "On it you shall not do any work, you or your son or your daughter or your male servant or your female servant, or your ox or your donkey or any of your livestock, or the sojourner who is within your gates, **that your male servant and your female servant may rest as well as you.**" (Deuteronomy 5:14, emphasis added). Thus, it's breaking the Sabbath to enjoy rest while having people work for you. So, for example, that rules out going out to eat at restaurants and thus paying cooks and servers to prepare and serve you food on the Sabbath. As believers we should desire all people to come to the knowledge of the Lord and the joy of His commandments, including the Sabbath. What kind of witnesses would we be if we teach obedience to God's commandments while directly participating in someone's violation of those same commandments?

Some people might feel overwhelmed at the idea of keeping the Sabbath. We're all very busy, and keeping the Sabbath takes some getting used to. Just have faith in God. The Bible says "in plowing time and in harvest time" we are to rest on the Sabbath day (Exodus 34:21). That is to say, God understands that we're busy and have a million things to do, but that's no excuse for not resting on this day. Whatever's going on in your life, He's got it. All you have to do is trust that He knows best and be faithful to what He has told you to do. And don't worry, it gets easier with practice. Soon you'll find yourself looking forward to the Sabbath every week.

Fellowship with Other Believers

We are instructed in the Torah to have a holy gathering on the Sabbath (Leviticus 23:3), which is why we see in Scripture that it was Yeshua's and the apostles' custom to attend synagogue and worship with others on this day (Luke 4:16; Acts 13:14, 42, 44; 16:13; 17:1-2; 18:4). Therefore, make every effort to fellowship with likeminded believers on the Sabbath. If there aren't any Messianic or Sabbath-keeping Christian congregations near you, perhaps have a home group meeting with friends and family. You can study the Bible together, sing worship songs, and encourage one another in the Lord.

As the author of Hebrews says, "Let us consider how to stir up one another to love and good works, **not neglecting to meet together**, as is the habit of some, but encouraging one another, and all the more as you see the Day drawing near" (Hebrews 10:24-25, emphasis added). God intended the Sabbath to be a joyful time for believers to encourage each other and celebrate all that He has done for us.

Don't Buy or Sell

We are prohibited from buying and selling on the Sabbath day (Nehemiah 10:31), so make sure you go grocery shopping and take care of errands during the other six days of the week. The Sabbath is a special day of rest and a time to spend with God, family, and friends. Therefore, it shouldn't be treated like the other days of the week on which "common" things are done—that is, chores, errands, shopping, etc.

Reflect on the Gospel

One of the reasons God gave us the Sabbath day is to remind us of our deliverance from Egypt:

> You shall remember that you were a slave in the land of Egypt, and the Lord your God brought you out from there with a mighty hand and an outstretched arm. **Therefore the Lord your God commanded you to keep the Sabbath day.** (Deuteronomy 5:15, emphasis added)

God rescued us from harsh slavery and gave us the gift of physical rest. Since Egypt is often used to refer to sin throughout the New Testament, we can see how on a spiritual level the Sabbath is a prophetic picture of our salvation in the Messiah. Yeshua rescued us from the slavery of our sins and gave us true rest in Him.

Thus, one of the best ways to keep the Sabbath is by remembering that we were once enslaved to our sins, but now we are free because of Yeshua. We can do that by reading through New Testament passages about Messiah or simply praying and reflecting on the impact of the Gospel in our lives—our deliverance from our own "Egypts"—and resting in God's love.

Observe Sabbath Traditions

The Jewish people have been keeping the Sabbath for thousands of years and thus have developed many meaningful traditions that are worth exploring and implementing into your Sabbath observance. One of the most common traditions is to light the Sabbath candles. Two long candles are used. The light from the candles reminds us that we are to be a light to the nations. Traditionally, the female head of the household will light the candles just before sundown Friday evening and then recite the following blessing:

HEBREW:

Baruch attah Adonai Eloheinu melech ha-olam asher kideshanu, bemitzvotav vetzivanu lehiyot or lagoyim v'natan lanu et Yeshua Meshicheinu or ha-olam

ENGLISH:

Blessed are you, Lord our God, King of the universe, who sanctifies us with his commandments and commanded us to be a light to the nations and who gave to us Yeshua our Messiah the Light of the world.

In addition, it is customary to drink wine on the Sabbath. At sunset on Friday evening, a blessing is recited over the wine—this is called the *kiddush* ("sanctification")—in order to express the sanctity of the Sabbath. Wine "gladdens the heart of man" (Psalm 104:15) and therefore is a fitting beverage to enjoy on the most joyful day of the week. The blessing over the wine goes like this:

HEBREW:

Baruch attah Adonai Eloheinu melech ha-olam borei p'ri hagafen

ENGLISH:

Blessed are you, Lord our God, King of the universe, who creates the fruit of the vine.

Another common tradition is to make *challah*, which is special braided bread. The challah symbolizes the manna from heaven. It reminds us that God is our provider. Indeed, just as God provided for the Israelites in the wilderness by giving them manna, we can rest assured that He will provide for our needs. After saying the blessing over the wine, a blessing is said over the challah:

HEBREW:
Baruch attah Adonai, Eloheinu melech ha-olam hamotzi lechem min ha-aretz

ENGLISH:
Blessed are you, Lord our God, King of the universe, who brings forth bread from the earth.

Just as we mark the beginning of the Sabbath with special prayers and traditions, we do the same at the end of the Sabbath with a *havdalah* ceremony. Havdalah means "separation"; it represents the point at which the weekly Sabbath is officially concluded on Saturday night and thus separate from the other six days of the week.

To begin the havdalah ceremony, we pour wine into a glass to the point that it overflows onto the plate underneath, symbolizing our hope that the joy of the Sabbath will flow into the upcoming week. Then we light the havdalah candle, which is a special candle with six strands braided together, symbolizing how we are to carry the light of the Sabbath into the upcoming week. After the candle is lit, a blessing is said over the wine—the same blessing said at the beginning of the Sabbath.

The second part of the ceremony involves the enjoyment of fragrant spices. These spices (usually cloves or cinnamon) are commonly kept in a special decorated box. A blessing is said over the spices and then the box is passed around to everyone at the table. The sweet aroma of the spices reminds us of the Sabbath joy that lingers with us even as we go about our week. The blessing over the spices goes like this:

HEBREW:

Baruch attah Adonai Eloheinu melech ha-olam borei minei v'samim

ENGLISH:

Blessed are you, Lord our God, King of the universe, who creates varieties of spices.

The third part of the ceremony is the blessing over the light of the havdalah candle. After the blessing is said, it is customary for everyone to lift their hands towards the flame. The shadows that are cast from our hands remind us of the separation between light and darkness and our duty as disciples of Yeshua to separate the holy from the common just as we separate the Sabbath from the other six days of the week. The blessing over the light of the havdalah candle goes like this:

HEBREW:

Baruch attah Adonai Eloheinu melech ha-olam borei me'orei ha'esh

ENGLISH:

Blessed are you, Lord our God, King of the universe, who creates the light of the fire.

The final blessing is the havdalah blessing, which is said over the wine. After the blessing is said, the flame of the candle is extinguished with the spilled wine on the plate. The havdalah blessing is as follows:

HEBREW:

Baruch attah Adonai Eloheinu melech ha-olam hamav'dil bein kodesh l'chol bein or l'choshech bein Yisraeil la'amim bein yom hash'vi'i l'sheishet y'mei hama'aseh baruch atah Adonai hamav'dil bein kodesh l'chol

ENGLISH:

Blessed are you, Lord our God, King of the universe, who divides between holy and profane; between light and dark; between Israel and the nations; between the seventh day and the six days of work. Blessed are you, Lord, who divides between holy and profane.

Observing these traditions is a wonderful way to make the Sabbath day special for you and your family. In addition to observing Jewish tradition, you can also come up with your own traditions. Some families might have a family game night on Friday nights or go for walks in the park on Saturday afternoons. The Sabbath is a God-focused and family-focused time, so whatever you do, make sure it revolves around the theme of the day—spending time with God and family.

Find Delight in the Sabbath

God did not intend the Sabbath to be a burden, but rather a time of joy. The Bible says that blessings come when we honor the Sabbath and call it a delight (Isaiah 58:13). Yeshua said the Sabbath was made for our benefit (Mark 2:27). So enjoy it and give thanks to God for giving us rest.

CHAPTER 2
PASSOVER

Let the people of Israel keep the Passover at its appointed time.
Numbers 9:2

One of the most important annual events on the Hebrew calendar is the Passover meal and the seven-day Feast of Unleavened Bread. This powerful biblical holiday commemorates the Exodus story—the deliverance of Israel from their slavery in
ancient Egypt.

The story of Passover is recorded in the Book of Exodus. It takes
place in Egypt, where the people of Israel were made to work as slaves.
One day the Israelites cried out to God for deliverance, so God sent
Moses to go to the ruler of Egypt, Pharaoh, and order him to let the
Israelites go free. Pharaoh refused, so God sent plagues upon the land
of Egypt: frogs, locusts, and boils, among others (Exodus 7-10). But
even after suffering these plagues, Pharaoh still refused to let the Israelites go.

Since Pharaoh continued to stubbornly resist God's will, God told
Moses that He was going to send one last plague upon the land—the
death of the firstborn son in every home in Egypt. However, God provided a means of safety for the Israelites. He told Moses that He would
not touch the houses that had the blood of a lamb on their doorposts.
So Moses told the Israelites to kill a lamb and spread its blood on the
doorposts of their houses, and thus those houses were "passed over" by
God and spared from the plague.

After suffering through this terrible plague, Pharaoh finally agreed to let the Israelites go free, and all of God's people quickly followed Moses out of Egypt. However, after a short while, Pharaoh ordered his army to go after them, and they chased the Israelites to the bank of the Red Sea. God split the sea, creating a path for the Israelites to cross. But after they crossed, the Egyptian army continued to chase them. So God caused the sea to crash down on the Egyptians, covering them in the water.

Thus, the Israelites were delivered from Egypt and began their journey to the Promised Land. And the Feast of Passover was established to commemorate this miraculous story.

How is Passover Relevant to Christians?

The simplest answer to this question is that God commanded His people to keep Passover and Unleavened Bread throughout their generations as a statute forever (Exodus 12:14). Thus, if you consider yourself a follower of the God of Israel, this is something you are to do forever.

Also, during the last supper before His crucifixion, Yeshua told His disciples to "do *this* in remembrance of me" (Luke 22:19, emphasis added). What were they doing when Yeshua said that to His disciples? If we look a few verses earlier, we see that they were doing a Passover seder. Indeed, if you are a follower of the Messiah, you are to do Passover in remembrance of Yeshua.

Not only is Passover commanded by God and reiterated by Yeshua, but even the apostle Paul tells Christians to observe this feast:

> Cleanse out the old leaven that you may be a new lump, as
> you really are unleavened. For Christ, our Passover lamb, has
> been sacrificed. **Let us therefore celebrate the festival**, not

with the old leaven, the leaven of malice and evil, but with the
unleavened bread of sincerity and truth. (1 Corinthians 5:7-8,
emphasis added)

So the simple answer is that God repeatedly told us to observe
Passover and then reiterated that command through Messiah and the
apostle Paul. Therefore, Passover is relevant to Christians. But it goes
much deeper than that. The story of Israel's deliverance from Egypt is
a prophetic picture of our own deliverance from our slavery to sin. It's
all about the Gospel. Thus, the story of Passover is our story too. And
God wants us to always remember this story. He wants us to always
reflect on His love for us and that He gave His Only Son so that we
can be free.

The following are some ways you can celebrate this amazing feast day.

Eat Unleavened Bread

In the Torah we are instructed to eat unleavened bread for seven
days. Why did God give us this strange commandment? The Bible
actually gives us one of the reasons in Deuteronomy:

Seven days you shall eat it with unleavened bread, the bread of
affliction—for you came out of the land of Egypt in haste—
that all the days of your life you may remember the day when
you came out of the land of Egypt. (Deuteronomy 16:3)

The Israelites didn't have time for their bread to rise when they left
Egypt since they had to leave "in haste," so we see here that the purpose
of eating unleavened bread is to help them recall their deliverance—
that is, the day they came out of Egypt. God wants us to remember
that the basis for our relationship with Him is that He delivers us (Ex-

odus 6:2-8). We have done nothing to earn His love. He "heard the groaning of His people" and acted simply on the basis of His great love. Eating Unleavened Bread is a tangible reminder of that.

Remove the Leaven from Your Home

During the days leading up to Passover, we are to remove all of the leaven (*chametz*) from our homes (Exodus 12:15). Leaven is a substance that is added to dough to cause it to ferment and rise. In the Bible, leaven is often symbolic of sin. Thus, the command to remove leaven from our homes is designed to teach us to examine our hearts. It is a time of introspection. As we explore every corner of every room in our homes for literal leaven, we are to ask God to search every corner of our hearts to reveal any sin in our lives.

On the day before Passover, it is customary to do a final search around the house for leaven. This is called *bedikat chametz*, which means "search for leaven." For fun, parents usually hide a few pieces of leavened bread around the house so that their children will have something to find. It is customary to turn off all the lights in the house and use a candle or flashlight during the search. The candle or flashlight represents Yeshua, who is "the light of the world" (John 8:12). It's by His light that we can overcome sin in our lives. A blessing can be said before beginning the search:

HEBREW:

Baruch attah Adonai Eloheinu melech ha-olam asher kidishanu, bemitzvotav vetzivanu al bi'ur chametz

ENGLISH:

Blessed are you, Lord our God, King of the universe, who has sanctified us with his commandments, and commanded us concerning the removal of chametz.

After leaven is found, the children are to call for their father to come and sweep it up. This teaches us that we are unable to remove sin from our lives on our own. We need our Father in heaven's help. Once all the leaven is found, it is gathered together to be burned or thrown away. This symbolizes how Yeshua frees us from sin and removes it from our lives.

In addition to removing literal leaven, some people might remove anything that could potentially cause spiritual corruption in their homes. Do you have old movies, music, or books that cause you to stumble in your walk of holiness? If so, this is the season to finally throw those things away. Unleavened Bread is a time to be intentional about getting rid of any baggage that might be holding you back. "A little leaven leavens the whole lump" (Galatians 5:9).

Review the Exodus Story

The story of Israel's deliverance from Egypt is to be remembered and retold at the time of Passover every year:

> **Remember this day** in which you came out from Egypt, out of the house of slavery, for by a strong hand the Lord brought you out from this place. (Exodus 13:3, emphasis added)

> And when your children say to you, 'What do you mean by this service?' you shall say, 'It is the sacrifice of the Lord's Passover, for he passed over the houses of the people of Israel in

Egypt, when he struck the Egyptians but spared our houses.'
(Exodus 12:26-27)

You shall tell your son on that day, 'It is because of what the
Lord did for me when I came out of Egypt.' (Exodus 13:8)

We can learn many lessons from the Exodus story and what it
means to us as Christians today. The Exodus teaches us about standing on God's promises in the face of extreme opposition. It teaches
us that, in the midst of the plagues and trials of life, God is with His
people. Most importantly, it teaches us about our own personal salvation in Yeshua.

The command to remember and retell this story can be fulfilled
in many ways. You could read through the book of Exodus and have
Bible studies with friends or family. You and your family could watch
movies about the Exodus story. (I recommend watching movies *in addition to*, not as a replacement of, reading the biblical narrative.) Also,
in the Passover *haggadah*, there is a section of the seder where you retell
the Exodus story and allow the kids to ask questions about the various
traditions involved in the celebration.

Do a Passover Seder

One of the most significant parts of the celebration is the Passover
seder. This is a special ceremony that kicks off the seven-day festival of
Unleavened Bread. During the seder, we eat special foods that help us
reconnect with the Israelites' journey out of Egypt and recall our own
spiritual journey out of sin. A haggadah (telling) is a book or an outline
used to set forth the order of the ceremony. You can look to join a local
Messianic or Christian congregation's Passover seder, or simply get a

haggadah and do your own with your family and friends. (See our website for a haggadah that you can use: www.freedomhillcommunity.com.)

Some of the traditional foods on the seder plate include the following:

Karpas – *Parsley. This represents the growth of the Israelites and God's blessing on them as promised to Abraham. Near the beginning of the seder, the karpas is dipped in salt water and eaten. The salt water reminds us of the tears that were shed in Egypt because of the harsh slavery and oppression of God's people. In addition, it reminds us of the pain and sorrow that come as a result of our sin, and of our separation from God before we met Yeshua our Messiah.*

Maror – *A bitter herb, such as horseradish. This represents the bitterness of slavery and reminds us of the bitterness that comes as a result of our sins.*

Charoseth – *A mixture of apples, nuts, and honey. This represents the mortar that the slaves in Egypt used to make bricks. It reminds us of the sweetness of God's grace.*

Matzah – *Flat, unleavened bread. This represents the bread made by the Israelites when they left Egypt. They didn't have time for their bread to rise because they left "in haste" (Deuteronomy 16:3). This is to help us recall our deliverance from Egypt and remind us that we need to get the leaven (sin) out of our lives.*

Ze'roa – *A roasted lamb shank bone. This represents the Passover sacrifice whose blood was spread over the doorposts of the Israelite homes in Egypt. It also represents the Messiah Yeshua, the lamb of God who takes away the sin of the world.*

Wine/Grape Juice – The wine is representative of the blood of Yeshua that was shed for us (Matthew 26:27-28). Four glasses of wine are drunk during the seder. These glasses stand for the four "I will" promises found in Exodus:

> Say therefore to the people of Israel, 'I am the Lord, and I will bring you out from under the burdens of the Egyptians, and I will deliver you from slavery to them, and I will redeem you with an outstretched arm and with great acts of judgment. I will take you to be my people, and I will be your God, and you shall know that I am the Lord your God, who has brought you out from under the burdens of the Egyptians.' (Exodus 6:6-7)

1) **The cup of Sanctification – "I will bring you out."**
2) **The cup of Deliverance – "I will deliver you."**
3) **The cup of Redemption – "I will redeem you."**
4) **The cup of Praise – "I will take you to be my people."**

In addition to the four glasses of wine representing the four promises of God in Exodus 6:6-7 is the Cup of Elijah. This glass of wine is poured toward the end of the seder, and it helps us recall the prophecy that Elijah must return to prepare the way for the Messiah. This glass is filled and then left on the table. Then one of the children opens the front door of the house in order to symbolically "welcome" Elijah to come.

Interestingly, both the Jewish people and Christians are waiting for the return of the Messiah. The Jewish people are waiting for what they believe to be the first coming of Messiah, while Christians are waiting for the Second Coming. This part of the seder is a great moment to include a prayer for the salvation of the Jewish people and everyone else who doesn't yet know Yeshua as the Messiah.

Other meaningful traditions are performed throughout the seder, such as the lighting of candles and the washing of hands. But perhaps the most interesting tradition is the search for the *afikomen*. As part of the seder, matzah is kept in a special covering with three compartments representing the triune nature of God—Father, Son, and Holy Spirit. One piece of matzah is placed in each compartment. In Judaism, the three pieces of matzah are said to represent Abraham, Isaac, and Jacob. The middle matzah represents Isaac, the son of Abraham, who willingly submitted to his father to be a sacrifice (Genesis 22). This is a beautiful picture of Yeshua, the Son of God, who willingly laid down His life for us.

Just as Yeshua was broken for our transgressions (Isaiah 53:5-7), the middle piece of matzah is broken in two. One half of the broken matzah is placed back into the covering while the other half is wrapped in a separate linen cloth. This piece is called the afikomen, which means, "that which comes after," or "dessert." The afikomen is then hidden. This represents Yeshua's body on earth. After He was crucified, his body was wrapped in cloth, and then He was hidden away in the tomb (Matthew 27:59-60). Toward the end of the seder, the children search for the afikomen, and whoever finds it gets a reward. The reappearance of the afikomen of course represents the resurrection of the Messiah.

The seder concludes with a celebration in which everyone shouts, "Next year in Jerusalem!" This is done in anticipation of the coming of our Lord when we will have the Passover meal with Him in His kingdom.

Observe the High Holy Days

During Unleavened Bread are two "high Sabbaths": one on the first day and the other on the last day of the festival. Just like the regular weekly Sabbath, these are days on which we are not to do any work (Leviticus 23:7-8). Instead we are to simply enjoy God's gift of rest and reflect on the meaning of this special time of year. We are also commanded to have a holy convocation on these two days, so plan ahead to be in fellowship with other believers at those times. Unleavened Bread is a great opportunity to get together with your congregation or small group of friends to have a Bible study, play games, or worship the Lord through music and dancing.

Eat Awesome Food

You might feel limited in what you can eat due to having to avoid anything with leaven, but there are a lot of great Passover recipes to enjoy. Traditional foods include things like Matzah Ball Soup, which is a mixture of matzah meal, eggs, water, and chicken fat. Another favorite is Baklava, which is a pastry made with thin layers of unleavened dough, honey, and nuts. Indeed, your *chametz* fast doesn't have to be miserable. Look up new recipes to try—you might be surprised at how many great ideas there are!

CHAPTER 3
SHAVUOT

You shall observe the Feast of Weeks.
Exodus 34:22

The feast of Shavuot—better known as Pentecost—is one of the most amazing events on the Hebrew calendar. In biblical times, Shavuot marked the beginning of the new agricultural season. It was called *Chag HaKatzir*, which means "The Harvest Holiday." It is also known by the name, "The Feast of Weeks."

According to Jewish tradition, it was during Shavuot when the God of Israel betrothed His people at Mount Sinai. Marriage vows were given when the people spoke as one, saying, "All the Lord has spoken, we will do" (Exodus 19:8). And the marriage contract, or *ketubah*, was written down in the form of the Torah. In the New Testament, the outpouring of the Holy Spirit upon Yeshua's disciples also occurred on Shavuot (Acts 2). This festival therefore celebrates true, biblical worship. Indeed, God gave both the Truth of His Word (Torah) and His Spirit on Shavuot, thus enabling His people to worship in Spirit and Truth: "God is spirit, and those who worship Him must worship in Spirit and Truth" (John 4:24).

The feast of Shavuot, along with the rest of God's feasts, is called an "appointed time" (Leviticus 23:2). It is a special time that God told us to remember and celebrate every year—kind of like a wedding anniversary. Therefore, you can be sure that when God's people come together for this special celebration, the God of Israel will show up in a powerful way. He scheduled these appointments with us in His Word, and He never misses them.

The following is a list of ways that you can make this amazing holy day part of your life.

Count the Omer

One interesting thing that God told His people to do is count fifty days from the first fruits offering given at the time of Passover to the feast of Shavuot (Leviticus 23:15-16). This is called the counting of the omer. An omer is a unit of dry measure equal to one tenth of an ephah (half a gallon dry measure). In biblical times, an omer of barley was brought to the Temple on each of the days leading up to Shavuot and then waved before God.

At this time there is no physical Temple in Jerusalem, so we cannot go to the Temple and wave the omer before God like they did in biblical times. But we can still count the days to Shavuot. In Judaism, it is customary to recite a Hebrew blessing each evening during the counting of the omer. It goes like this:

HEBREW:
Baruch ata Adonai Eloheinu melekh ha-olam asher kid'shanu b'mitzvotav v'tizivanu al sefirat ha'omer

ENGLISH:
Blessed are you, Lord our God, King of the Universe, who has sanctified us with your commandments and commanded us to count the omer.

In addition to the traditional blessing, some people like to make an omer calendar for the family. Each evening you can have a special moment where you mark the days and count as a family. You can even pick out memory verses for the children to recite. There are a lot of creative ways to fulfill this mitzvah.

Give an Offering to the Lord

Three times a year God's people are commanded to come before the Lord, and we are told not to come empty-handed. Shavuot is one of those times:

> Three times a year all your males shall appear before the Lord
> your God at the place that he will choose: at the Feast of
> Unleavened Bread, at the Feast of Weeks, and at the Feast of
> Booths. They shall not appear before the Lord empty-handed.
> (Deuteronomy 16:16)

One way to do this would be to give a special offering to your local congregation, a charity, or a ministry of your choice that aligns with the heart and vision that the Father has given you. This is one simple way to honor the spirit behind this particular commandment on a practical level.

Give a "Wave Offering"

According to the Torah, we are to bring two loaves of bread to be waved as an offering to the Lord on Shavuot:

> You shall bring from your dwelling places two loaves of bread
> to be waved, made of two tenths of an ephah. They shall be of
> fine flour, and they shall be baked with leaven, as firstfruits to
> the Lord. (Leviticus 23:17)

These two loaves of bread represent the Ten commandments that were written down on two stone tablets. They also symbolize the two "testaments" (Old and New) coming together as one. Simply have your community leader—or if you are the head of your household, you can do this with your own family—wave the two loaves of bread sometime during your celebration. They are to be waved in every direction before the Lord as a public declaration of God's provision.

Bless the Poor

In connection to Shavuot is also a command to leave the edges of your field unharvested for the poor:

> And when you reap the harvest of your land, you shall not reap your field right up to its edge, nor shall you gather the gleanings after your harvest. You shall leave them for the poor and for the sojourner: I am the Lord your God. (Leviticus 23:22)

Therefore, leading up to Shavuot, you should be looking for ways to minister to the poor. For instance, congregations or home groups could have a special donation box dedicated specifically for benevolence. You could also do a canned food drive or even pick a day to help your local food pantry or soup kitchen. Just as in Acts 2 God sent His comforter—the Holy Spirit—on Shavuot we are to help comfort others.

Renew Your Marriage Vows

Since Shavuot traditionally represents a wedding ceremony between God and Israel, many couples use this time to renew their marriage vows and recommit their hearts to both one another and their King. There are many creative ways to do this, and it can be as simple or elaborate as you'd like. You can go all out and have a big "wedding celebration" or simply gather your children and friends together in your living room to be witnesses while you and your spouse recite your marriage vows to each other.

Read the Book of Ruth

During the season of Shavuot, it is customary to read *Megilat Rut*, the Book of Ruth. In the Bible, Ruth was a Moabite woman who had such a love for her Hebrew mother-in-law, Naomi, that when Ruth's husband died, she decided to become part of God's people and follow the God of Israel. This book is read during Shavuot because the story takes place during the harvest season, and also because Ruth's "grafting in" to the people of Israel reminds us of the first Shavuot when Israel accepted the Lord and became His people at Mount Sinai.

As followers of Messiah, the book of Ruth also reminds us of our own acceptance of Messiah Yeshua whereby we became "fellow citizens with the saints and members of the household of God" (Ephesians 2:19).

Decorate Your Home and Congregation

Another fun tradition is to decorate your home or congregation with fresh greens and flowers. This serves as a reminder of God's wisdom and character contained in the Torah given at Shavuot, and how it is a "tree of life" to those who hold fast to it (see Proverbs 3:18). Children can also make necklaces and bracelets out of flowers and wear them during the celebration.

Have a Community Baptism

Many believers will hold a community baptism as part of their celebration. This ceremony symbolizes the death, burial, and resurrection of Messiah Yeshua. When we get baptized, we are illustrating our identification with Messiah—being buried with Him by being immersed in water, and resurrecting with Him as we come out of the water:

> Do you not know that all of us who have been baptized into
> Christ Jesus were baptized into his death? We were buried
> therefore with him by baptism into death, in order that, just as
> Christ was raised from the dead by the glory of the Father, we
> too might walk in newness of life. (Romans 6:3-4)

Baptism also symbolizes repentance—leaving behind our old life and being made into a new creation (2 Corinthians 5:17). It is a public declaration of our commitment to Yeshua and a life led by Spirit and Truth.

Keep a Day of Rest

Shavuot is a "high sabbath." Like the regular weekly Sabbath, it's a day of rest on which we are not to do any regular work. It is also a "holy gathering" (Leviticus 23:21). Thus, if at all possible, make every effort to be part of a congregation of likeminded believers on Shavuot. If there is no congregation in your local area, and you simply aren't able to travel to one, get together with just a small group of family, friends, or perhaps your Bible study group to give honor to the Father on this very special day.

This should be a day of praise and worship to our King. It's a day on which we're commanded to "rejoice" (Deuteronomy 16:11). So, whether you are by yourself, in a small home group, or a part of a larger congregation, celebrating Shavuot is not only good for your soul, but it also brings God's people together to worship our King.

Eat Shavuot-Themed Food

It is customary to eat dairy during Shavuot, such as cheesecake and ice cream. Why? Because God brought His people out of Egypt in order to bring them into a "land flowing with milk and honey" (Exodus 3:8-17). Therefore, eating dairy commemorates the sweetness of the new life that lies before us when Yeshua returns and brings us all into His Kingdom.

CHAPTER 4
YOM TERUAH

It will be to you a day for blowing trumpets.
Numbers 29:1

D id you know that God commands us to rejoice and make noise? Indeed, Yom Teruah—also known as the Feast of Trumpets or Rosh HaShanah—is an incredible celebration during which believers come together to worship the God of Israel with shouts of joy and the blast of the shofar as we look forward to the second coming of our Messiah, Yeshua (Jesus).

Yom Teruah marks the beginning of the fall feasts. The name *Yom Teruah* literally means, "Day of Shouting/raising a noise." This day has later become known as Rosh HaShanah, which means "head of the year." It is the beginning of the civil year on the Jewish calendar. According to Jewish tradition, Rosh HaShanah is an anniversary commemorating the creation of Adam and Chavah (Eve). It is a day to reflect on our special relationship with the God of the universe and recommit to walking in our created purpose—that is, sanctifying the name of God in this world and bringing Him glory.

The following is a list of ways that you can make this amazing holy day part of your life.

Observe the Season of Teshuvah

On the Hebrew Calendar, the month before the fall feast days is called *Elul.* In Judaism, this month is traditionally associated with the theme of repentance, or in Hebrew, *teshuvah*. It's a time of introspection, reconciliation, and preparation. The season of teshuvah begins at the beginning of Elul and goes all the way to Yom Kippur. It is traditional during this season to blow the shofar and recite Psalm 27 every morning.

The word teshuvah literally means to "return." The goal of this entire season is simply to return to God—in other words, to restore unhindered fellowship with Him. According to tradition, there are four steps of teshuvah. The first step is to acknowledge and forsake your sin. This season is a time of introspection. We are to ask God to search our hearts and reveal to us anything that offends Him. Ask yourself these questions: Do I really know Yeshua personally? Do I truly love God with all my heart, mind, soul, and strength? Do I truly love my neighbor as myself? Am I offending God by what I do, think, or say?

As God reveals sins in your life, the first step is to forsake them. You have to truly desire to give them up. This is a difficult task for many people. It can result in an identity crisis as we begin to give up destructive habits and deep-seated character deficiencies from which God wants to deliver us. Nevertheless, it's worth it for the sake of having unhindered fellowship with God.

The second step of teshuvah is to regret your transgressions against God. Our King desires humility and honesty. When we feel sorrow for hurting our spouse, parents, or close friends, they should be able to see our sincerity. If we've deeply hurt someone, it's not enough just to say, "Sorry." Sometimes we have to fall on our knees. Sometimes we have to allow our eyes to shed tears. Regretting our transgression is a crucial step toward restoring a relationship.

If we do this with each other, how much more should we with God? When we pray and ask God for forgiveness for our sins, we should be sincere. We might consider physically bowing down and displaying genuine humility and regret for our offenses. Indeed, Scripture says that the sacrifices of God are a broken spirit and a contrite heart (Psalm 51:17). The season of teshuvah is a time to just be real. Being open and honest with your emotions might be difficult, but it's important for healing and growth.

The third step is to confess our transgressions and make amends with those we've hurt. Scripture says that when we confess our sins, God will forgive us and cleanse us from all unrighteousness (1 John 1:9). Nothing is more liberating than "coming clean." Confessing your sins to God and others is an essential step of teshuvah.

The Bible says that confession and prayer bring healing (James 5:16). Healing also comes by making amends with those we've sinned against (Matthew 5:23-24). We can acknowledge that we've hurt others all day long, but until we actually do something about it, it's basically meaningless. As James says, "Faith without works is dead." Therefore, as much as possible, we must pursue to make things right with our fellow man. If you've sinned against your wife, you should bring home some flowers and a card. If you've sinned against your husband, you should make him his favorite meal for dinner. We must do what we have to do to make amends. That's what this season of teshuvah is all about.

The fourth and final step is to accept God's forgiveness and move forward in faith. The problem that many people face when it comes to teshuvah is that they don't follow through to this final step. People will often get stuck in regret and never move forward. Satan tries to twist our emotions and use them against us to lead us to self-condemnation and depression. He knows that if he can keep us from moving forward, we will be rendered useless to God's Kingdom.

Don't believe Satan's lies. When you received the Lord, you were adopted into God's family. Your Father loves you and is always willing to forgive you when you turn back to Him. The apostle Paul assures us of this in the book of Romans:

> There is no condemnation for those in Christ Jesus.
> (Romans 8:1)

Biblical teshuvah requires pressing on toward the goal. Therefore, we must accept our forgiveness and our identity as a child of God and disciple of Yeshua. We must walk in faith and allow ourselves to be comforted by the divine presence of God.

Blow the Shofar

In Leviticus 23:24, we are told that Yom Teruah is a memorial proclaimed with a "blast of trumpets." The Hebrew word translated "trumpet" is *shofar*, which is an ancient musical instrument made of a ram's horn. Our Yom Teruah celebration should consist of making lots and lots of noise with the shofar! As believers in Messiah, the shofar blast is done in anticipation for the second coming of Yeshua, who will return at the sound of a "trumpet" (1 Thessalonians 4:16). In addition, it is a call to teshuvah (repentance) as Yom Teruah is the first of the "Ten Days of Awe" leading up to Yom Kippur.

Don't Do Any Ordinary Work

Yom Teruah is called a day of rest. It is a "high Sabbath." Therefore, no work is to be done on this day (Leviticus 23:25). This is definitely something to keep in mind as we make plans with our employers to request time off from work a few weeks in advance. This is an easy *mitzvah* (good deed) to do on Yom Teruah. We simply enjoy God's gift of rest—and remember the ultimate rest we have in our Savior, Yeshua (Matthew 11:28).

Have a Holy Convocation

Yom Teruah is all about community. Therefore, if at all possible, we are to make every effort to be part of a congregation of likeminded believers on this special day. If there is no congregation in your local area, and you simply aren't able to travel to one, then get together with just a small group of family, friends, or perhaps your local Bible study group. Together with other believers, enjoy the many fun traditions attached to this feast and make this a day of praise and worship to our King.

Have a Tashlich Ceremony

Tashlich is a beautiful tradition. On the afternoon of Yom Teruah, God's people gather together to throw breadcrumbs or small rocks into a river (or any other flowing body of water). This tradition symbolizes God's forgiveness through Yeshua and how He casts our sins into "the depths of the sea," as mentioned in the book of Micah:

> Who is a God like you, pardoning iniquity and passing over transgression for the remnant of his inheritance? He does not retain his anger forever, because he delights in steadfast love. He will again have compassion on us; he will tread our iniquities underfoot. **You will cast all our sins into the depths of the sea.** (Micah 7:18-19, emphasis added)

Since Rosh HaShanah is regarded as the head of the year, this is also a great time to make "New Year's Resolutions." The month of Elul leading up to the fall feasts is supposed to be a time of introspection. In fact, in Aramaic, the word Elul means to "search." During this season of teshuvah, we are to ask God to search us and expose anything in our lives that offends Him. Therefore, your breadcrumbs or small rocks can represent particular sins, addictions, or even certain character deficiencies (e.g. tendencies to be prideful or easily frustrated). This tradition symbolizes the act of throwing those things away and allowing God to work in your life and change you.

Read the Story of the Binding of Isaac

It is customary on Yom Teruah to read and reflect on the binding of Isaac (Genesis 22). God commanded Abraham, "Take your son, your only son Isaac, whom you love, and go to the land of Moriah, and offer him there as a burnt offering on one of the mountains of which I shall tell you" (Genesis 22:2). This is the first mention of the word *love* in the Bible, and it is connected to the picture of the Father offering His only Son:

> For God so loved the world that He gave His only Son, that whomever believes in Him should not perish but have eternal life. (John 3:16)

The blowing of the shofar on Yom Teruah reminds us of how God provided a ram in Isaac's place as an offering to God (Genesis 22:13). As believers in Yeshua, it also reminds us of how the Messiah died in our place to free us from the death we deserve because of our sins. Many Messianic pictures are found throughout this incredible story. Here are some of the interesting parallels that exist between Yeshua and Isaac: (1) both had a miraculous birth (Genesis 21:1-7, Matthew 1:18-25); (2) both were the "only son" of their fathers (Genesis 22:2, John 3:16); (3) both carried the wood for their own sacrifices (Genesis 22:6, John 19:17); and (4) both were delivered from death on the third day (Genesis 22:4, 1 Corinthians 15:4). These are just a few examples out of many.

Eat a Festive Meal

Last but not least, no feast day is complete without having a *feast*! On Yom Teruah, it is customary to eat apple slices dipped in honey, symbolizing our hopes for a "sweet" new year. For believers in Yeshua, eating honey-dipped apples is done in anticipation for when Yeshua returns at the sound of a trumpet and brings His people into a "land flowing with milk and honey."

CHAPTER 5
YOM KIPPUR

It is a Sabbath of solemn rest to you, and you shall
afflict yourselves; it is a statute forever.
Leviticus 16:31

Out of all of the appointed times that God told us to remember and observe, Yom Kippur—the Day of Atonement—is regarded as the most important of them all. The name Yom Kippur means "Day of Atonement." It is the day when the High Priest went into the holy of holies and performed specific rituals in order to atone for the nation of Israel (Leviticus 16). According to Jewish tradition, Yom Kippur recalls the day when the people of Israel sinned against God by making the Golden Calf. God forgave the people of their sin after Moses made intercession on their behalf (Exodus 32-33). This pattern is clearly seen throughout the rituals of Yom Kippur as the High Priest intercedes for Israel and asks for God's forgiveness every year on this day. And we see this exact pattern again as we look to our heavenly High Priest, Yeshua (Jesus), who is "able to save completely those who come to God through Him, because He always lives to intercede for them" (Hebrews 7:25).

Ultimately, Yom Kippur is a day to reflect on the Gospel. God gave His only Son to become a sacrifice that would atone for our sins. And indeed, Yeshua is our High Priest who makes intercession for us in the heavenly tabernacle. Hallelujah!

The following is a list of ways that you and your family can observe this most holy day.

Ask for Forgiveness

The time between Yom Teruah and Yom Kippur is known as the Ten Days of Awe. It is a time of repentance and asking forgiveness—of God *and* our fellow man. As we see in Scripture, forgiveness is extremely important to God. This is the time to really take it seriously.

If you need to ask someone for their forgiveness, but you feel like they won't be receptive, do it anyway. Swallow your pride. Just call or write them and apologize. Yes, it might be uncomfortable and they might not be happy that you've contacted them, but at that point you've done all you could. It's out of your hands. Once you reach out to them and sincerely apologize, it's up to them to follow through with obeying the Bible's commandment to forgive. Your role is simply to do the right thing regardless of how they respond.

Forgive Others

Along with asking for forgiveness, you must also be willing to forgive others. Indeed, the biggest stumbling block to asking for forgiveness *and* giving forgiveness is pride. Just let it go. You simply don't have the right to hold a grudge. As Yeshua beautifully illustrated in His parable of the Unforgiving Servant (Matthew 18:21-35), our Master has forgiven us a tremendous debt that we could never pay. Therefore, who are we to not have mercy on our fellow servant?

> For if you forgive others their trespasses, your heavenly Father will also forgive you, but if you do not forgi ve others their trespasses, neither will your Father forgive your trespasses. (Matthew 6:14-15)

Keep a Day of Rest

We are commanded to not do any work on Yom Kippur (Leviticus 23:28). The Bible calls it a "Sabbath of solemn rest." Make sure you request time off from your job on this important day so you can completely focus on God.

Fast

God commands us to afflict ourselves on Yom Kippur (Leviticus 16:31). Several passages in the Bible connect this phrase to fasting. "I afflicted my soul with fasting" (Psalm 35:13). Indeed, the connection between Yom Kippur and fasting became so established in Judaism that, by the time of the First Century, the day was simply called "the Fast" (Acts 27:9).

Afflicting our souls through fasting is an act of complete humility and self-denial. At a fundamental level, it takes our focus off of ourselves. When we fast, we are choosing to deny ourselves a basic human enjoyment in order to fulfill God's purposes. It reminds us that this life is not about us, but about Him. Moreover, fasting on Yom Kippur is a practical way to emulate Yeshua who said, "Man shall not live by bread alone, but by every word that comes from the mouth of God" (Matthew 4:4).

If you are pregnant or have health problems that might prevent you from abstaining from food on Yom Kippur, then that is certainly understandable. A greater *mitzvah* than fasting is the preservation of life. If that's the case, pick something other than food that you can fast from for the day.

Have a Holy Convocation

Yom Kippur is a community event (Leviticus 23:27). Make every effort to be part of a congregation of likeminded believers on this day.

Most Messianic and some Christian fellowships hold beautiful prayer services on Yom Kippur that you can be part of. If you don't have a local fellowship, plan ahead to travel to one and observe this holy day with other believers. Also, it's traditional to come to Yom Kippur service dressed in white clothing.

Read the Book of Jonah

On Yom Kippur it is customary to read the book of Jonah. This is an incredible story that teaches us about God's forgiveness and mercy. Jonah was a righteous prophet who ran away from God's commandment to go to Nineveh. Ultimately, Jonah's attempt at escape was unsuccessful as he was thrown into the sea and swallowed by a great fish. Three days later, Jonah was released from the fish, and he journeyed to Nineveh to prophesy against them. Amazingly, through Jonah, one of the biggest revivals in history took place as the entire nation of Nineveh came to repentance.

From the story of Jonah we learn that we are unable to escape God. We've all sinned and fallen short of His glory. We all must face this reality. Jonah also teaches us that, no matter our past sins, God will have mercy on us when we repent. God declared that Nineveh was to be destroyed because of their wickedness, yet He forgave them when they acknowledged their wicked ways and made teshuvah.

The most convicting part of the story is Jonah's attitude throughout the book and especially in the last chapter. The author ironically paints the main character, Jonah, the prophet of the Lord, as the "bad guy" and the people of Nineveh as the "good guys." First, Jonah runs away from the mission that God gave him. Then after God gives him a second chance, he curses God for showing mercy to the nation of Nineveh. God's plan for His people is that we are to be a light to the nations, yet Jonah's bitterness toward the Ninevites hindered him for rejoicing in seeing God's plans accomplished. The bottom line of the story is not whether you are a prophet of God or a Ninevite, but whether you repent of your sin. Does your heart break for what breaks God's heart? Do you love people like God loves them? The story is meant for us to ask these questions, which makes it a fitting story for Yom Kippur.

Not only is Jonah an amazing story of repentance and forgiveness, but it's also prophetic. Yeshua said that Jonah is a sign to confirm that He is the Messiah. Just as Jonah was in the belly of the fish for three days and three nights, Yeshua was in the heart of the earth for three days and three nights (Matthew 12:40).

Have a Joyous Celebration

At the end of Yom Kippur, we blow the shofar (ram's horn) and celebrate! God has forgiven our sins! Indeed, Yeshua's atoning work on the cross assures us of forgiveness when we repent (1 John 1:9). Once the sun sets, feel free to break your fast with a celebratory meal. If you're able to be part of a local fellowship, have a praise and worship service with music and dancing. This exciting celebration extends all the way through the Feast of Sukkot.

CHAPTER 6
SUKKOT

You shall keep the Feast of Booths seven days.
Deuteronomy 16:13

The feast of Sukkot, more commonly known as the feast of Tabernacles, marks the end of the biblical fall feasts. It's the most joyous celebration on the Hebrew calendar as God's people come together and celebrate before the Lord in anticipation for the return of the Messiah and the wedding supper of the Lamb.

The name Sukkot means "booths," and it comes from the mitzvah to dwell in booths during the seven-day festival (Leviticus 23:42). This mitzvah recalls the forty years during which the Israelites dwelled in booths as they wandered the desert after their deliverance from Egypt. It's also known as the feast of ingathering (Exodus 23:16), or simply "the feast" (1 Kings 12:32). Sukkot celebrates the gathering of the harvest at the end of the agricultural year in Israel, prophetically symbolizing the day when all of God's people are gathered together in the Kingdom at the Second Coming of Yeshua.

While we can't know for sure, some have speculated that the American holiday of Thanksgiving was originally inspired by Sukkot. It's also believed that Sukkot was the time of Yeshua's birth—thus, if that's true, followers of Yeshua have another reason to rejoice during this time!

The following is a list of ways that you can celebrate this amazing festival.

Dwell in a Sukkah

One of the commandments of Sukkot is to dwell in a *sukkah* during the days of the festival (Leviticus 23:42). A sukkah is a temporary dwelling place like a fort or a tent. Traditionally, it has at least three walls and must be built under an open sky. Many people decorate their sukkah with lights, pictures, and even vegetables like pumpkins. It is customary to use branches and leaves as part of the roof of the sukkah. This is so you can see the stars through the roof at night and reflect upon God's glory and majesty:

> When I look at your heavens, the work of your fingers, the
> moon and the stars, which you have set in place, what is man
> that you are mindful of him, and the son of man that you care
> for him? (Psalm 8:3-4)

To dwell (Hebrew: *yashav*) in the sukkah literally means to "sit," and it can consist of simply spending time in the sukkah during the day, reading scripture, praying, or even sleeping in it at night. Many people will invite friends and family to share meals inside of the sukkah. Recently, among several Messianic and Christian groups, it has become traditional to organize a camping trip during the feast where families will camp in tents, build a community sukkah, and live in community for the week.

Wave the Lulav and Etrog

In the Torah we are commanded to take "the fruit of splendid trees, branches of palm trees, and boughs of leafy trees and willows of the brook, and [...] rejoice before the Lord [our] God seven days" (Leviticus 23:40). Traditionally this has come to be observed by waving the *lulav* and *etrog*. The lulav is a collection of plants that are tied together in a bouquet, and the etrog is a citron, which is a fruit similar to a lemon. The Bible gives no explanation for this strange mitzvah, but it's something that God tells us to do during this time—therefore, as obedient children, we carry out this mitzvah out of love for our Father in heaven.

Some commentators have suggested that the etrog represents a heart and the lulav represents a backbone. Thus, the person who has a true heart for God will be given a "spiritual backbone." Perhaps carrying out this mitzvah purely out of a heart to obey God is a means by which God strengthens our spiritual backbone—that is, by waving the lulav and etrog, we are walking by faith and not by sight. We are obeying God even when we don't understand. After all, if we can't obey God in the simple things, what's to say that we would obey Him with regard to the difficult things?

Rest on the First and Eighth Day

During Sukkot are two high Sabbaths—the first day of the festival and the "eighth day" that directly follows the seven days of Sukkot—on which we are not to do any work (Leviticus 23:35-36). These are days to simply enjoy God's gift of rest as we remember the ultimate rest we have in our Savior, Yeshua. We are also commanded to have a "holy convocation" on these two days.

Read the Book of Ecclesiastes

During the festival of Sukkot, it is customary to read the book of *Kohelet*, or Ecclesiastes. This book was chosen to be read at this time because its teachings relate much to the sukkah. Solomon, the author of Ecclesiastes, discusses how our physical world is temporal and fading away, just as the sukkah is merely a temporary dwelling that will come down at the end of the festival. Indeed, we do well to remember that the pursuit of pleasure and success in this life is ultimately meaningless, and true eternal fulfillment is found only in a relationship with God and keeping His commandments—"for this is the whole duty of man" (Ecclesiastes 12:13).

Give an Offering to the Lord

Sukkot is one of three times of the year when God's people are not to come before the Lord "empty-handed" (Deuteronomy 16:16). We are to bring an offering to the Lord, thanking Him for His love and provision. One way to honor the spirit behind this particular commandment on a practical level would be to give a special offering to your local congregation, a charity, or a ministry.

Give to the Poor

In addition to family and friends, we are told to include "the fatherless and widow who are within your towns" in our celebration (Deuteronomy 16:14). Thus, it has become customary to look for ways to minister to the poor and needy during Sukkot. Just as Sukkot symbolizes God dwelling with man, may we bring the light of Yeshua into people's lives through spending time, listening, giving, and loving them.

Celebrate Messiah's Birth

As Christians begin to discover the value of God's feast days, they tend to no longer see a need to celebrate non-biblical holidays like Christmas. However, that certainly doesn't mean we shouldn't celebrate the birth of our Messiah! On the contrary, Sukkot is the perfect opportunity to celebrate Yeshua's birth. In his paper, "Why I Don't Celebrate Christmas," Messianic Theologian Tim Hegg says this:

I celebrate the birth of Messiah as never before, but I have come to understand that Christmas and the birth of Messiah have nothing in common. Contrary to the popular Christmas carol, Christ was not born on Christmas day. I personally feel that the Festival of Booths (Sukkot) is best suited to remember the "dwelling of God with man," both historically and eschatologically. I have found it very encouraging, while sitting in the Sukkah, to consider the love of God displayed in sending His own dear Son to dwell with me in my humble and temporary abode. What is more, Sukkot adds to the celebration of Christ's incarnation the hope of His future dwelling upon the earth, a time when all the nations will celebrate the festival.[9]

One of the ways we can celebrate Yeshua's birth during Sukkot is to sing "Christmas songs" that have to do with Messiah. Again, just because we don't celebrate Christmas anymore doesn't mean we have to throw out powerfully anointed songs about our Lord and Savior that have come to be associated with Christmas. Sukkot is a fitting time to reclaim those songs for our Messiah's glory.

The Eighth Day

The great eighth day, known as *Shemini Atzeret*, is connected to— yet distinct from—the seven-day feast of Sukkot. The eighth day represents new beginnings and symbolizes the world to come in which we'll spend eternity with our Father in heaven. Scripture refers to this time as "the new heavens and new earth" that will be established after Messiah's

---

9   Tim Hegg, *TorahResource*. "It is Often Said: Two Thousand Years of Christianity Cannot be Wrong!" www.torahresource.com. Accessed 9/7/2016

thousand-year reign on earth (Revelation 21-22). As mentioned earlier, this day is a high Sabbath on which no work is to be done.

Simchat Torah (rejoicing in the Torah) is observed as part of the eighth day. In traditional Jewish and Messianic synagogues, the Torah scroll is paraded around while everyone dances and sings. The one-year reading cycle of the Torah concludes on the eighth day, so it's customary to physically roll the Torah scroll back to the beginning in order to go through the cycle all over again in the upcoming year.

Rejoice

The most important mitzvah during the feast of Sukkot is the command to *rejoice*:

> **You shall rejoice** in your feast, you and your son and your daughter, your male servant and your female servant, the Levite, the sojourner, the fatherless, and the widow who are within your towns. (Deuteronomy 16:14, emphasis added)

Regardless of our role, social status, or life circumstances, Sukkot is a time to be happy and rejoice. What reason do we have to rejoice? On the most basic level, we are to rejoice because of God's provision. In ancient Israel, Sukkot celebrated the gathering of the harvest at the end of the agricultural year. If you are reading this right now, it means you're alive. That means that God has sustained you to this point with enough food and drink. He has provided—thus, you have a reason to rejoice!

In addition to God's physical provision, Sukkot is a celebration of the Gospel message. Sukkot comes right after Yom Kippur, which is a commemoration of how God gave His only Son to atone for our sins. On the basis of Yeshua's death and resurrection, we are able to take part in the Wedding Feast of the Lamb. Sukkot—specifically the eighth day—represents that wonderful time when we'll be with God in the world to come:

> Behold, the tabernacle of God is with man. He will dwell with them, and they will be his people, and God himself will be with them as their God. (Revelation 21:3)

If you've received Yeshua as your Savior, you are invited to dwell—that is, to tabernacle—with our great God. Isn't that reason enough to rejoice?

CHAPTER 7
HANUKKAH

At that time the Feast of Dedication took place at Jerusalem.
John 10:22

H anukkah, also known as the Feast of Dedication or the Festival of Lights, is a holiday commemorating the rededication of the second Temple. It is a celebration of faith and uncompromising commitment to God's Word as we remember the Maccabean revolt during which a small Jewish army fought against the forces of evil in their day and took back the Temple, cleansing it and rededicating it to God.

In 167 BCE, the Syrian king, Antiochus IV—one of the successors of Alexander the Great—began harshly oppressing the Jewish people. He outlawed the study of the Torah, banned observance of the weekly Sabbath and biblical feasts, and even ordered women who circumcised their sons to be thrown from the top of the city wall (2 Maccabees 6:1-11). The holy Temple was desecrated through drinking parties and prostitution. Antiochus even went so far as setting up an altar to Zeus in the Temple and ordering pigs to be sacrificed on it (1 Maccabees 1:46-59).

Eventually the oppression and persecution of the Jewish people led to a revolt. In 165 BCE, a small army of faithful Jewish believers successfully forced the Syrian-Greeks out of Israel and took back the Temple. Thus, they began the process of cleansing the Temple and rededicating it for proper worship of the Lord. Hanukkah is a time to remember and celebrate this victory of truth and faithfulness to God's Word. In addition, as followers of Yeshua (Jesus), we reflect on the Gospel message during this festival. Just as God worked through a small group of Jewish believers to take back the holy Temple, Yeshua took back our personal "temples" from the enemy and dedicated us to God.

Hanukkah is the Hebrew word for *dedication*. This eight-day festival is about a *dedicated* people who refused to compromise. Today, the world around us is demanding that we compromise the Word of God. It demands that we not only accept their blatant defiance and hatred of God, but also that we celebrate it. As we observe Hanukkah, we remember that we are to stand strong against the forces of compromise.

Yeshua Himself celebrated Hanukkah. The Gospel of John records that Yeshua went to the Temple for the Feast of Dedication (John 10:22-23). Therefore, as followers of Yeshua, it is fitting for us to follow His example by celebrating this feast too. The following is a list of ways you can celebrate Hanukkah today.

Learn About Hanukkah and What It Means Today

The story of Hanukkah can be found in the books of First and Second Maccabees. Many lessons can be learned from the story that apply to us as believers today. First and foremost, the story of Hanukkah teaches us about standing firm on God's truth in the midst of extreme opposition. In our modern culture of compromise, this is a message we desperately need to be reminded of often.

The Bible says that God is light, and in Him is no darkness at all (1 John 1:5). We are told that we are liars if we claim to have fellowship with God and yet walk in darkness (1 john 1:6). As we celebrate Hanukkah—the festival of "lights"—we are reminded that we're in a spiritual battle. The story of Hanukkah encourages us to be faithful to God and refuse to allow any darkness into our lives. Hanukkah is a reminder to be a light to the nations by expressing the love of Yeshua and reaching out to the lost, showing them that there is a better way.

We can also look at Hanukkah as a time of introspection. When the Temple was liberated, they had to cleanse it for proper worship. This was a process. Every nook and corner had to be searched and cleansed. In the same way, we can ask the Lord to search our own personal "temples" this Hanukkah season. May we be delivered from the obvious sins in our lives, and may the Lord also search us completely and cleanse us from the deep-seated idolatry that is hidden deep in our hearts. Hanukkah is the perfect time to rededicate your life to God.

There are many other lessons we can learn from the Hanukkah story. Study, pray, and ask God to teach you.

Light the Hanukiah

The hanukiah is a special, nine-branched candelabra used for Hanukkah (not to be confused with the seven-branched menorah in the Temple). The middle branch stands higher than the other eight and is called the *shamash* (servant) candle. The shamash candle is used to light the other candles.

On each night of Hanukkah at sundown, a new candle is lit. Traditionally, on the first night, one candle is placed on the rightmost branch of the hanukiah. The shamash candle is then lit and used to light the first candle. On the second night, another candle is added to the right end of the hanukiah. The shamash candle then lights the candles left to right (the newest candle is lit first). A new candle is added each night and the process is repeated until the eighth night when all nine candles on the hanukiah are lit.

On each night of Hanukkah, after the lighting of the candles, the following blessings are recited:

HEBREW:

Baruch attah Adonai Eloheinu melekh ha-olam, asher kideshanu bemitzvotav ve-tsivanu lehiyot or le-goyim v'natan-lanu et Yeshua Meshicheinu or ha-olam.

ENGLISH:

Blessed are You, Lord our God, King of the universe, who sanctified us with His commandments, and commanded us to be a light to the nations and Who gave us Yeshua our Messiah the Light of the world.

HEBREW:

Baruch attah Adonai Eloheinu melekh ha-olam, she'asah nisim l'avoteinu, b'yamim haheim bazman hazeh.

ENGLISH:

Blessed are You, Lord our God, King of the universe, who made miracles for our forefathers in those days at this time.

A third blessing is recited only on the first night of Hanukkah:

HEBREW:

Baruch attah Adonai Eloheinu melekh ha-olam, shehekheyanu, v'ki-yamanu vehegianu lazman hazeh.

ENGLISH:

Blessed are You, Lord our God, King of the universe, who has kept us alive, sustained us and brought us to this season.

It's traditional to let the light from the hanukiah shine for everyone to see. So after you light the candles each night, place the hanukiah in your window where the lights can clearly be seen from the outside. Yeshua said that we are the light of the world, and a city on a hill cannot be hidden (Matthew 5:14). Displaying your hanukiah is a simple way to literally "let your light shine" as a reminder of the Lord's calling on your life to be a light to those around you. Plus, it's a great conversation starter for your neighbors!

Play the Dreidel Game

The dreidel is a spinning top with four sides. On each side is a Hebrew letter: Nun, Gimmel, Hey, or Shin. These letters are an acronym for the phrase, *Nes Gadol Hayah SHam*, or in English, "A great miracle happened there." In Israel, the letter Pei is used instead of Shin, making the acronym, *Nes Gadol Hayah Poh*, "A great miracle happened here."

To play the game, players sit in a circle, and each person gets an equal amount of candy pieces or coins. They begin by all placing something into the pot in the center of the circle. Then each player takes a turn spinning the dreidel. Each side of the dreidel tells the player whether they are to put in or take from the pot. If it lands on a Gimmel, the player gets the entire pot. If it lands on a Hey, the player gets half of the pot. If it lands on a Shin, the player has to put into the pot. And if it lands on a Nun, nothing happens and it just goes to the next player. The game ends when someone has all the candy pieces or coins.

Eat Hanukkah-Themed Foods

No feast is complete without having a *feast*! Traditional Hanukkah foods include *sufganiyot*, which are deep-fried jelly doughnuts, and *latkes*, which are fried pancakes made from grated potatoes and served with applesauce and / or sour cream. It's customary to eat fried foods during Hanukkah in remembrance of the miracle of oil recorded in later rabbinic tradition. It is said that at the time when the Jewish people were rededicating the Temple, there was enough oil to light the menorah for only one day. Yet, that little bit of oil lasted for an entire eight days, which was enough time to prepare more oil to keep the menorah continually burning in the Temple:

> When the Greeks entered the Temple, they polluted all the oils in the Temple, and when the Hasmonean dynasty overcame and defeated them, they checked and they found but one cruse of oil that was set in place with the seal of the High Priest, but there was in it only [enough] to light a single day. A miracle was done with it, and they lit from it for eight days. (Shabbat 21b)

In addition to fried foods, many people like to make Hanukkah-themed snacks like cookies baked in the shape of dreidels, hanukiahs, etc. It's customary to invite friends and family over for dinner during Hanukkah. All the foods, symbols, and traditions of the holiday provide a great opportunity to share about the meaning of Hanukkah and how God is awesome.

Be Happy

According to tradition, Hanukkah is a time to praise God and be thankful:

> The sages fixed those days, making them holidays for praise and thanksgiving. (Shabbat 21b)

As believers, we have so many reasons to be happy. Hanukkah is the perfect opportunity to celebrate and praise God for all He has done in our lives. The Bible says, "Happy are you, O Israel! Who is like you, a people saved by the Lord" (Deuteronomy 33:29a). Yeshua saved us, delivered us from our enemies, and dedicated us to God. Hallelujah!

CHAPTER 8
PURIM

*These days of Purim should be observed at their appointed seasons, as
Mordecai the Jew and Queen Esther obligated them.*
Esther 9:31

The feast of Purim commemorates the deliverance of the Jewish people from the evil Prime Minister Haman's conspiracy
to destroy them. It's a celebration of God's love and protec-
tion in the midst of a hostile world.

The story of Purim is recorded in the Book of Esther. It takes place
in the ancient Medo-Persian empire at the time when the seventy years
of exile had come to an end and the Jewish people were allowed to go
back to Jerusalem (Jeremiah 29:10). While some of the Jews returned
to the Promised Land, many stayed in Persia.

The story begins with Ahasuerus, the King of the Medo-Persian
empire, removing Vashti as queen and choosing Esther (Hadassah), a
young Jewish woman, to replace her. Shortly after Esther was crowned
queen, her cousin Mordecai, one of the King's servants, hears about
a plot to assassinate King Ahasuerus. He reports it to Esther, who in-
forms the King, thus saving the King's life.

At that time lived an evil prime minister of the empire by the name
of Haman. The King ordered his servants to bow before Haman and
pay homage to him, so all of them did ... except for Mordecai. When
Haman heard about Mordecai's refusal to bow before him, he schemed
to destroy Mordecai, along with all of the Jewish people in the land
(Esther 3:8-11).

When Queen Esther learned of Haman's plans, she called for the Jewish people to fast on her behalf. She courageously approached King Ahasuerus concerning Haman's evil conspiracy against her people. Because of Esther's bravery, Haman was sent to the gallows, and the Jewish people were permitted to defend themselves against those in the empire who sought to do them harm.

In remembrance of the miraculous events that took place, Queen Esther and Mordecai established the observance of Purim to celebrate all that God had done for His people (Esther 9:20-32).

How is Purim Relevant to Christians?

Since Purim is a Jewish holiday, it's often asked whether or not believers in Yeshua should celebrate it. The answer is yes! First, it's in the Bible. And according to the apostle Paul, "all scripture is breathed out by God and profitable for teaching, for reproof, for correction, and for training in righteousness" (2 Timothy 3:16). The book of Esther is included in "all scripture." Second, if you love the God of Israel and stand with the Jewish people, then Purim is for you:

> Therefore they called these days Purim, after the term Pur [...] the Jews firmly obligated themselves and their offspring **and all who joined them**, that without fail they would keep these two days according to what was written and at the time appointed every year. (Esther 9:26-27, emphasis added)

Indeed, "all" who stand in solidarity with the people of Israel are invited to join them in observing Purim. So here are some ideas on how believers today can celebrate this amazing feast.

Learn About Purim and What It Means Today

The best place to start is to read through the book of Esther. It doesn't take long. Set some time aside to read through the book either on your own or with your family.

The book of Esther teaches us many lessons about God's faithfulness to His people and how He keeps His promises. It teaches us about the power of fasting and prayer. It teaches us that God can use us in amazing ways if we dedicate our lives to Him. Read through Esther and ask God to give you revelation about His character and will for your life.

Fast the Day Before Purim

This fast is known as *Ta'anit Ester* (Fast of Esther), and it commemorates the three-day fast observed by the Jewish people just before Queen Esther spoke to King Ahasuerus about Haman's evil plans. Traditionally, the fast begins the day before Purim at sundown and ends at the beginning of Purim at sundown.

Fasting and prayer are great ways to connect to the story of Purim on a practical level by doing what the ancient Jews did in the events leading up to their deliverance. As Christians, we can also connect our fast to the Gospel and our deliverance from sin as we pray for the salvation of the Jewish people and anyone else who doesn't know Yeshua as their Messiah.

Make Purim Baskets

Another Purim tradition is *Mishloach manot*, or the "sending of portions." It is derived from Esther 9:22, which says, "They should make them days of feasting and gladness, and sending portions of food to one another, and gifts to the poor." This tradition is observed by making baskets containing food, candy, or small gifts. The baskets are usually decorated and then delivered to friends and family on Purim day.

Give to the Poor

Part of the celebration of Purim includes giving generously to the poor (Esther 9:22). Prayerfully seek the Father's will on how to apply this part of the feast. Meeting the needs of the poor is very close to the Father's heart, and the feast of Purim is certainly a wonderful opportunity to minister to the poor and needy.

Have a Costume Party

It's traditional to dress up in costume for Purim. This tradition comes from Esther hiding her Jewish identity from King Ahasuerus per Mordecai's instructions at the beginning of the story. Kids love putting on costumes, so you could have them dress in royal attire as kings and queens to help them connect to the story.

The Bible says, "So I commend the enjoyment of life, because there is nothing better for a person under the sun than to eat and drink and be glad. Then joy will accompany them in their toil all the days of the life God has given them under the sun" (Ecclesiastes 8:15). Purim is supposed to be fun and joyful. And for many people, dressing up is simply a way to have fun and enjoy the holiday.

Tell the Story of Esther

On the Feast of Purim it's customary to read the *Megillat Ester* (Scroll of Esther) in front of your congregation, synagogue, or Bible study group. You can make this as interactive and fun as you'd like! What a lot of people do is give the children noisemakers and sit them up front so they can "boo" and yell when the name Haman is mentioned and cheer when they hear the name Mordecai.

The tradition of drowning out the name of Haman is based on Deuteronomy 25:17-19, which tells us that we are to "blot out the name of Amalek." It is believed that Haman was a descendant of Agag, the King of Amalek. So according to the sages, we fulfill the mitzvah to blot out the name of Amalek by making so much noise when Haman's name is mentioned during the reading of Esther that his name is "blotted out."

Eat Purim-Themed Food

It's traditional to have a special meal with friends and family during Purim. Some traditional foods include a large challah with raisins. It's also customary to eat meals made with beans and peas. And the most famous Purim dish is *hamantashen*, which are triangular cookies filled with jelly or fruit.

ABOUT FREEDOM HILL COMMUNITY

Learning His Ways. Living His Word. Sharing His Truth.

F reedom Hill is a Messiah-centered community of believers and media-driven ministry based in St. Charles, MO. We are devoted to proclaiming the Gospel of Yeshua (Jesus) and pursuing the roots of our Christian faith. We follow the Scriptures and encourage individuals and families to live for Yeshua with a foundation of the Spirit and the Truth.

In light of our passion to pursue the roots of our Christian faith, one of our goals is to help our Christian brothers and sisters rediscover the beauty and value of the Torah. Why? Because Torah observance is an important part of the life and message of our Messiah. It was prophesied that the Messiah would "elevate the Torah and make it honorable" (Isaiah 42:21). Indeed, Yeshua rested on the Sabbath every seventh day, kept the biblical feast days, and didn't eat unclean animals. The word *Christian* literally means "Follower of Christ." As Christians, we are to walk as Yeshua walked (1 John 2:6). Since Yeshua kept and taught the Torah, it is appropriate for us to do the same.

In addition, the original Christian movement that emerged out of Yeshua's teachings continued to keep the Torah throughout the New Testament. In fact, Yeshua's instructions to His disciples just prior to His ascension were to make disciples of "all the nations" and teach them all that He had commanded them (Matthew 28:19-20). The

New Covenant established by Yeshua is intended to write the Torah on our hearts through the work of the Holy Spirit (Jeremiah 31:33). Thus, a return to a Christianity as originally taught and practiced by Messiah and the apostles must include a desire to keep the Sabbath, feasts, and dietary instructions in the Torah.

But where do we begin in reaching our Christian brothers and sisters with these truths? As a ministry, our plan is simply to continue developing resources—everything from simple introductions to the Sabbath and feasts to deeper biblical studies on these important truths and how to defend them. In addition to this book, we have a growing library of articles and sermons available for free on our website. Our teachers and pastors speak about these topics every week at our local congregation as well as at Christian/Messianic conferences and congregations throughout the United States.

If God puts it on your heart to partner with us in carrying out this vision, we could use your support in the following ways. First, we ask that you keep us in prayer. Pray that God will continue to guide and direct our steps. Second, we ask that you consider donating to Freedom Hill Community. You can give online through a one-time donation or set up a recurring monthly donation on our website (**www.Freedom-HillCommunity.com**). Personal checks can be made out to Freedom Hill Community and mailed to the following address:

Freedom Hill Community
P.O. Box 1865
St. Charles, MO 63302-1865

Third, please spread the word about Freedom Hill Community. Sign up to our newsletter on our website so you never miss an update.

Share our articles and videos on social media. Consider inviting one of our teachers to come speak at your congregation.

Your support makes it possible for us to share the Gospel of Yeshua and the Torah with people around the world. Thank you for partnering with us in reaching the nations.

Made in United States
Troutdale, OR
09/20/2023

13045247R00054